This publication is designed to provide accurate and authoritative information in regard to the subject matter covered. It is sold with the understanding that neither the author nor the publisher is engaged in rendering legal, accounting, tax, or other professional service. If legal advice or other expert assistance is required, the services of a competent professional person should be sought.

The information provided in this book is intended to be helpful in providing a course of action in the often difficult process of the short sale. Every situation is unique. Before attempting a short sale you are advised to seek the counsel of a competent real estate attorney and accountant.

Neither the publisher nor author shall be liable for any loss of profit or any other commercial damages, including, but not limited to special, incidental, consequential, or other damages

The author specifically disclaims any liability, loss, or risk, personal or otherwise incurred as a consequence directly or indirectly of the use and application of any of the techniques or contents of this book.

From a declaration of principle jointly adopted by a committee of the American Bar Association and a committee of publishers.

Table of Contents

The Short Sale Handbook

OVERVIEW

We are currently living thru unprecedented times not seen in more than a generation. Our economy has been going thru one of the worst downturns in recent history. The basic elements of its foundations have been collapsing like dominoes. At the heart of this economic nightmare is a crisis in the housing market. A real estate bubble of unprecedented proportions has burst and everyone is running for the exit. This bubble was helped along in great part by the easy availability of credit. The race to gain market share by most of the major players in the mortgage industry, aided by the likes of Fannie Mae and Freddie Mac, and the securitizing of these mortgages brought about exotic, but very risky mortgage instruments. The huge inflows of capital from all over the world by parties participating in the highly profitable mortgage markets only intensified the problem. The over-supply of capital created an environment of easy money and caused increasingly relaxed underwriting standards. This in turn created the fuel that fed the bubble. Many unqualified individuals were now able to participate in the market. The purchasing power of both qualified and unqualified individuals was artificially augmented by complex instruments such as interest only ARMs and Option ARMs, otherwise known as "pick a payment loans". The combination of these factors helped to drive up housing demand to unprecedented levels. This sky-rocketing demand caused the elevation of prices in existing homes, and the rush to build new ones. In addition, the loose standards of equity requirements in the underwriting process, led to lending up to the full property value, and sometimes exceeding it. In most cases this leaves the lender with dangerous levels of capital at risk, and the homeowner trapped in situations where the property value has dropped below the balance of the loan, or combination of loans, on the property. This is what has become known as being "upside down" or "under water". It leaves the homeowner with no way out, and very few options.

When the market rolled over, the upward momentum all of the sudden was reversed. The market came crashing down almost in a straight and uncontrolled way. Property values have dropped in some areas as much as 50% or more, leaving many homeowners trapped equity wise, and unable to make the payments . At this point, the choices are few and painful.

You can opt to keep the property and keep making the payments on it, hoping that the value will come back some day. Depending on where the property is located this can be multiple years. Foreclosure or deed in lieu are two possibilities. These two will most likely bring about the worst repercussions in terms of credit damage and legal exposure. You can sell the property and make up the difference between the sales price, and the balance on all the loans in cash. This one is improbable in most cases because the sums of money that would have to be brought to closing would be prohibitive for most folks. Even for those who have the funds, the choice of whether to use their life savings to cover this deep hole without ever seeing the money again, would be a wrenching decision. The third option is the subject of this manual, and most likely the best option among a tough list of choices. You can say the lesser of all evils. We are talking about the short sale.

The short sale is a process by which a property is sold for a price below the amount that is owed on it. The entity that has a lien against the property agrees to receive funds in an amount short of the balance owed as a pay off. Therefore the term "short" sale. It sounds pretty simple. Getting to this point is the challenging part. It is usually a very straight forward process but only if done correctly. For the purposes of this book, the terms mortgagee will represent the current mortgage, and lien holder. Mortgagor refers to the individual or individuals obligated on the mortgage note. Lien holder refers to an entity holding a lien against the subject property. This book is meant for home owners who find themselves in this terrible situation as well as those who assist them as third party professionals.

Why is it the short sale best option in most cases? In general, it provides the best and most benevolent solution to the situation for all the parties involved. The credit and legal consequences to home owner are widely accepted as less harmful than a foreclosure, and a lot more feasible than a deed in lieu. It is also possible for the owner to obtain "debt forgiveness" for the difference between the loan balance and the net amount the lender receives, usually referred to as the deficiency. The lender (mortgagee) minimizes it's losses, by avoiding the expensive process of foreclosure, and the extreme costs of holding the property after the foreclosure takes place. Not to mention the unknown time frames and complications of reselling the property and the additional costs associated with it. In short, it is the quickest and least expensive option for the lender once it finds itself holding a non-performing loan. Remember that lenders are normally not willingly in the business of selling and managing real estate. They are in the banking / lending business. Any distressed real estate that they hold and manage after foreclosure is a burden on their balance sheets. Finally, buyers get a property at a great price and in most cases in much better condition than a property that has been foreclosed.

As mentioned before, the concept is straightforward. However, in reality the process could be full of challenges, and if not handled properly, probably destined for failure. If handled correctly and with a good dose of follow up, it will most likely lead to success, and great relief for the parties involved. The following pages give a description and provide a picture of the correct approach to a successful short sale.

PREPARATION FOR THE OWNER

In order to start the process, the current owner has to be able to present a case to justify the short sale request. It is in the best interest of the owner to show a convincing reason of why a short sale is the best alternative for the owner and the lender. One of the key elements will be to be able to show the financial picture of the current owner and how it relates to the short sale request. The lender(s) will also require a "hardship" letter from the owner explaining in relative detail the owner's current situation and the reason why the owner will not be able to maintain the property. Recently there has been lots of discussion as to the significance of hardship as a major factor as to the lender's (mortgagee) decision process. Especially when there is a large volume of cases that have to be processed, and the standardization that this is creating. There are also the cases where the mortgage is seriously delinquent even when the home owner might otherwise be in a good financial position. This is sometimes referred to as strategic default. Either way at this point, the specific hardship, and it's relation to the mortgagor's financial picture is still a crucial analysis point for the lender. It, combined with the other factors such as the eventual sales price and net revenue to the lender, will be key to the approval, and subsequent deficiency decision for the lender. Again, the overall financial situation of the obligated home owner(s) will be examined closely to determine if they qualify for this type of remedy. Another important element just alluded to, and arguably the most important, will be the value of the subject property. Usually a short sale is not an adequate solution to the lender unless the property's net value falls short of the amount(s) owed on the property. It directly affects the remaining amount owed after the sale takes place (deficiency). We will go into more detail about these elements and others later in the book.

PRELIMINARY RESEARCH

Proper preparation for the process of a short sale has to include a good dose of preliminary research. It is crucial to know the factors in the scenario you are working with. These will help to forecast the feasibility of the objective, and evaluate the odds of success or failure. Below are the most basic steps. Depending on the complexity of the situation, more research might be needed.

A. APPRAISAL OR BPO

The basis for the whole transaction will be the negotiated price and terms of the subject property. In order to ascertain the market value and possible sales price for the property, it would be a good idea to obtain an appraisal, or at the very least a Broker's Price Opinion (BPO), in order to place the property on the market at a price consistent with the short sale objective. This step will surely be repeated by the seller's lender, the mortgagee, in the processing of the request. It is imperative to obtain as accurate data as possible in order to eventually achieve a contract that will justify the short sale to all the parties involved. The average cost of an appraisal currently is around $350 to $400 for properties of less than $1 million. Properties above this price range usually cost more to appraise. You can also obtain the assistance of a qualified real estate agent who will research all the relevant comparables and narrow down a range of possible listing prices. Some lenders will require that an appraisal, BPO, or at least a certain number of comparables be submitted with the short sale request package.

B. TITLE SEARCH

It is advisable to conduct a title search in advance. This will show all the liens attached to the property, and other important issues related to the title. This simple and basic title work lessens the chances of having surprises at the last minute which could derail the deal. Title searches are normally conducted thru closing agents, title companies, or attorneys that usually handle real estate matters. Having a title search done prior to putting the property on the market will alert you to any potential problems or issues in this category, and give you time to address the matter. Prices vary depending on location, but generally, it is not very expensive.

C. PROPERTY CONDITION

A great number of short sales are conducted in "as is" condition. The reason is simple economics. The home owner is normally prohibited from receiving any monies related to the sale of the property. Since the mortgagee(s) is taking a loss on its loan, all possible funds (net of expenses) arising from the proceeds of the sale usually go to the mortgagee(s). If the seller / home owner is unlikely to recover any expenses for repairs, he or she is probably unwilling to consider paying for them. However, if the sale depends on minor repairs being done onto the subject property, then it might be in the seller's best interest to conduct such repairs in order to avoid losing the deal and possibly ending up in foreclosure. Every case is different. If the owner has enough funds available for repairs then it is an open option. However in most cases the home owner is unable or unwilling to do so. If the property is being sold "as is", it is important that the listing clearly states the fact in order to avoid delays or complete waste of time. It is also important to know that funds for repairs can also be negotiated with the buyer and mortgagee in the form of a credit at closing, a proportionate reduction in price, or other alternatives that can be mutually agreed to.

LISTING THE PROPERTY

Once the decision has been made to put the property up for sale at a price that will leave a net loss (short sale), the next step would be to list the property on the appropriate multiple listing system(s) and, or other informational networks indicating that it is a short sale. In some areas you might be able to list it without contracting with an agent by paying a fee to be able to list your property on that particular network. Listing the property is highly recommended since the property will be visible to thousands of potential buyers. Some real estate agents are working with clients that are just looking for opportunities like a good short sale. Many of these are "cash" buyers, who are the best suited buyers in many situations, but especially in a short sale since time is of the essence. Having a cash buyer could also be very advantageous while negotiating with the lender(s) because settlement could be done shortly after the lender accepts the short sale offer, and would not be subject to a mortgage approval process or an appraisal in order to obtain financing. In a declining market it would be in the best interest of the lender / mortgagee to sell as quickly as possible, since the next offer might be a lot lower than the current one, thus leaving a potentially larger loss for both the lender and the home owner.

In order to list the property you have to establish a "listing price". This is the price you are asking for in order to sell the property. As indicated before, you should evaluate sales figures in the subject property's market, of other properties that are comparable to yours, that have settled recently, and also check the listing prices of other comparable properties currently available for sale. Make sure they are the best comparable properties for yours. Take in consideration the location, neighborhood, style, size, number of bedrooms, bathrooms, property conditions, age, upgrades and many other factors. This will give you a very good idea of where to price adequately, and will present you with a good overall picture of the market trend. If you have obtained your own BPO or appraisal as recommended, you should have a good idea of what the listing price should be. The assistance of a good agent is highly recommended for this since agents have access to a very accurate database from which to obtain this critical information.

CONTRACT OFFERS

The short sale process, as far as the lender (mortgagee) is concerned, will technically start when an offer is made on the property. Due to the conditions previously described, the offer will give the lender a net amount which will be lower than the payoff on the mortgage (s). This will produce a net loss to the lender(s). These contracts are written in generally the same way as any other real estate contract except that they are adapted to the specific situation of a short sale, and with the understanding and agreement that the contract is subject to the lender (mortgagee), and any other applicable lien holder's acceptance. Also known as "third party approval". It should include the appropriate clauses, and allow for enough time for all the lien holders to process, evaluate, and make a decision on the offer.

In the event that multiple offers are made, the owner has to decide which is the strongest offer in very much the same way you would in a regular sale. The strongest contract offer is the one that has the best chance of getting accepted by the lender (mortgagee). The factors to consider include the net proceed to the lender (the higher the offer, the better chance to get it accepted), the down payment amount the buyer is willing to put down if he or she is getting financing, whether the buyer is requesting the seller, in this case the lender, to pay for all or part of the buyer's closing costs (this would result in a lower net yield to the lender), etc. Another factor to consider if you have multiple offers is if one of them is a cash offer. As noted earlier in the listing section, this type of offer is very compelling, especially if it's priced in a way that yields the same or higher net proceed to the lender (mortgagee), in comparison to the other contracts. However, if the cash offer is too low, it might be flat out rejected.

REASONABLE VALUE

To start evaluating the best priced offer, you obviously have to compare it to your listing price. In a stagnant or declining market, most likely, offers will come below your asking price. It is important to keep up to date on fluctuating values, especially in volatile markets. Keeping an eye on comparables is a must. The lender's analyst will be looking at that precise data as part of its decision making process. Unless you already have a good indication of the price tolerance of this lender, it is best to assume that they will not accept anything that is unreasonably lower than the current market value, unless the property condition or other factors command such a discount.   If the offer is too low, the lender will most likely turn it down thus wasting valuable time for all parties involved.

A. CASH CONTRACTS

As previously stated, cash contract offers have an obvious advantage over offers that are subject to financing, appraisals, or other financing related contingencies. Not only are they not dependent on these possible deal killers, but they can in effect go to closing in a much shorter period of time because of the lack of those financing hurdles.

If an offer price is in the acceptable range for the current lender, and it is paired with a cash contract, the odds of a positive decision are much improved. However, most cash buyers will usually bid less than others because they want an additional discount for their ability to close quickly and without too many complications, but sometimes their offer price is too low for the lien holder. There comes a point where the ability to close quickly is no longer worth the price. It is always advisable to have an idea of what those limits are before submitting a contract that is too low, and will waste valuable time. A good interaction with the loss mitigation department of the lender (mortgagee) will go a long way in helping to pinpoint those limits.

PREPARING THE NECESSARY DOCUMENTATION

In order to start the short sale process, the seller needs to prepare the documentation that will accompany the purchase offer that the lender will eventually be reviewing. This documentation includes, but is not limited, to financial statements, employment documentation such as paystubs and W2's, bank statements, and statements on other liquid assets such as stocks, bonds, etc. If the debtor-home owner is self employed, tax returns and profit and loss statements might also be required. If the owner(s) is unemployed, that too has to be documented. The previously mentioned hardship letter, detailing the reasons why the property owner cannot hold on to the property will also be required by the current owner's lender. Starting early on preparing all this documentation is very important since it might take some time to put together. Once an offer is received, time will be of the essence, and you don't want to be delayed waiting for this documentation to be organized.

CONTACTING THE BANK

The current owner's bank (mortgagee) needs to be contacted and advised that a short sale offer has been made. Establishing that particular bank's procedures for short sales is very important. Some lenders have their own particular procedures that need to be followed. As short sales become more prevalent, many lenders now require that their own forms and documentation procedures be used. Contact information, the names of the personnel involved are key to a smoother process. Building a professional rapport with these individuals could make the difference between a successful short sale transaction and an unsuccessful one. Time will be of the essence, and communication will become very important in order to achieve your ultimate goal. Constant follow up will be a must.

While getting to know the key people and procedures is important, finding out specific forms and type of documentation that this particular lender requires is also of great importance. Sending in the wrong form, or one not of their choice, can cause unnecessary and costly delays.

PUTTING TOGETHER THE SHORT SALE PACKAGE

An initial submission package has to be assembled and sent to the owner's lender (mortgagee) as soon as possible after an offer is accepted by the home owner(s). The package should contain all the basic documentation that this institution, (or institutions in the event of multiple lien holders) requires in order to start their evaluation process. Below is a list of basic documentation that needs to be submitted with the initial package. Please keep in mind that the short sale process is evolving substantially due to the current market conditions. It is always a good idea to consult with the lender as to what their exact documentation requirements before submitting the paperwork.

A. THE COVER LETTER

A clear, professionally written cover letter should headline the package. This letter should address the issue at hand directly by letting the lender know that the home owner is requesting to be considered for a short sale, and that the package accompanying the cover letter contains all the necessary documentation to initiate the review. Clearly state the reasons why the lender should consider a short sale instead of other options in the subject case. You must also brief the lender as to the reasons why the home owner finds it necessary to take this step (hardship, insolvency, property values etc.). The owner will most likely address and elaborate on those issues in the hardship letter. The cover letter is also the perfect place to emphasize to the lender(s) (mortgagee) that the home owner and mortgagor (not all home owners are obligated on the related mortgage) are requesting deficiency waivers as part of the short sale. We'll elaborate more on deficiencies ahead in the book. A second page can be included indicating the contact information for all the parties that will be involved in the process, including all lien holders, title company, home owner associations (if applicable), attorneys, as well as the buyer's and seller's agents etc.

B. AUTHORIZATION FORM FOR THIRD PARTIES

If acting on behalf of the home owner as a third party assisting in the process, an authorization from the home owner(s) and mortgagor(s) will be necessary, giving the necessary permission to transact the documentation and access private, confidential information. Most lenders and servicing companies have their own forms that they prefer to be used. In many cases, this form might have to be sent in, usually by fax, prior to starting the short sale process. Otherwise, the lender's representatives will not be able to communicate with anyone but the mortgagor(s). Thus potentially slowing the process down.

C. THE ESTIMATED SETTLEMENT STATEMENT (HUD 1) / NET SHEET

As stated above, the current lender and mortgagee will require certain documentation to ascertain the merits of the short sale offer. Knowing what documents will be needed and what the lender is looking for, will enhance the chances of an approval, and improve the turn time of the process dramatically. Most short sale departments will put aside files that have incomplete or erroneous documentation, thus causing major delays. Some institutions will even deny de short sale request, because the proper documentation was not included.

One of the documents that should be worked on first is the estimated settlement statement (HUD 1), also known as the net sheet. For those who are not familiar with this document, it shows the breakdown of all the numbers and details of the proposed transaction, and calculates the bottom line for all parties. The current lender (seller / mortgagee) will be looking closely at their net, and the items that lead up to it. These calculations are very important because they project what the lender will net, and therefore how much their loss will be. It will be a key part of the eventual minimum net (or max net loss) that this lender is willing to accept on the transaction. If your actual numbers come out short of this net amount at closing, the deal might fall apart. Please note that the same finalized document (HUD 1) will be used at closing as the official form that breaks down the numbers for all the parties involved. It will be reviewed and approved by all the parties, and signed by sellers and buyers as part of the closing transaction documentation.

One of the things to be aware of is that the current home owner (the mortgagor) is not allowed to receive any funds at closing, since the lender (the mortgagee) is taking a net loss on the deal.

It is not in the scope of this manual to teach how to complete a HUD 1 settlement statement. A sample of this document can be found in the exhibit section.

D. THE HARDSHIP LETTER

The mortgagee will require the mortgagor(s) to write a letter explaining the facts that have caused the situation to come to the point of having to let the property go, and why the mortgagee should accept the short sale proposal and take the related loss. The letter should be concise and to the point. One or two pages maximum. Honesty is the best policy. A lot of the follow up documentation that will be requested will also tell the story. It is better if both are in line with each other. If the letter paints a particular hardship, but the documentation provided indicates that no such hardship really exists, it might result in a flat out rejection, or an unfriendly counter offer.

E. FINANCIAL STATEMENT

All lenders (mortgagees) will request a financial statement showing the mortgagor's overall financial picture. Some lenders will have their own form they want filled out. Some will ask that you provide your own. If so, an excel type worksheet will do. The key components will be:

1) Income
   a) From employment / business
   b) Rentals
   c) All types of investments
   d) Retirement etc.
2) Expenses
   a) Revolving (i.e. credit cards and the like)
   b) Installment (car loans etc.)
   c) Real estate related expenses

     d) Utilities

     e) Food

     f) Gas

     g) Insurance

     h) Child support, Alimony

     i) Various living expenses (i.e. Dry cleaning etc)

     j) Miscellaneous expenses

3) Net loss or gain from income vs. expenses

4) Other real estate owned

5) Liquid funds

     a) Checking / Savings

     b) Investments (stocks, bonds, etc.)

     c) Retirement account (401K, IRA's etc.)

Remember that all the figures on the financial statement will be corroborated by the income documentation, credit report, and bank statements that will be requested. Again, it's a good idea that they be in line as much as possible.

F. PROFIT AND LOSS STATEMENTS (P&L)

For self employed individuals, and for commissioned related income, a Profit and Loss statement will be required. This P&L will need to cover certain periods. These requested periods will vary depending on the lender. The most common one will be the "year to date" or YTD P&L. For most self employed individuals there will be no pay stubs or other official income documentation during the current tax year. The YTD P&L will be used to calculate the average income for the period in question during the current business year. Also, if an extension was requested during the previous tax year, and no tax returns can be produced, a P&L for the entire year in question could be used in lieu of the subject tax returns, for income calculations.

G. TAX RETURNS

As mentioned before, most of the current lenders will require the tax returns for the previous two years for all those obligated on the note. These are used to help examine the overall financial picture of the individual(s). For most of those who are self employed, the examiner will use the two last tax returns and a YTD P&L, if applicable, to determine the average income for the periods in question. It also helps to produce a trend line for the income to see if it there is an indication of a dramatic reduction thus helping to explain a possible important factor that has brought about the short sale request.

It would be helpful if these calculations are done before submitting the short sale package since the income situation of the current mortgagors, together with the rest of their financial picture, will have a material impact on the decision by the loss mitigation department. Please remember that the appropriate department will verify the accuracy of any tax information submitted to them with the IRS. This is done with the mortgagors consent. This consent is usually requested by the mortgagee in writing by way of an official document designated by the IRS for this purpose. It is normally included as part of the initial short sale submission package. The form currently being used is known as form 4506 or 4506-T (see exhibits).

H. SUPPORTING DOCUMENTATION

Supporting documentation will be requested by the department dealing with the short sale request. In most cases, the file will not reach the case manager or other decision maker until the package is in order. The documentation required will be relative to the mortgagor's financial profile. It can include, but is not limited to pay stubs (the last two to four), the previous two years W2 forms, the two most recent bank statements and other liquid assets, evidence of other sources of income such as pensions, social security, unemployment etc. If the property is a homestead property, it needs to be documented. The most recent mortgage statements for all mortgage liens, HOA dues, and property tax bills, even when they are included in the monthly payment. Divorce and bankruptcy documentation, if applicable, needs to be provided also. Sometimes a copy of the executed listing agreement will be requested as well as two or three comparable sales records if available. As stated above, a form 4506 or 4506-T will also need to be submitted for tax verification purposes.

I. PAY OFF STATEMENT

A pay off statement is a document issued by the mortgagee's servicing department, or the respective lien holder's legal representative, showing the total amount of funds that it would take to completely pay off the current mortgage loan or other lien. The pay off figure is most likely to be different than the current balance. Some of the other factors that affect the pay off amount include (but not limited to):

- The current balance
- Interest accrued
- Administrative fees
- Penalties (if applicable)
- Escrow shortages / overages
- Any overdue payments

Pay off statements are only good thru a certain date. Normally, the exact date is noted on the statement itself. If that time period expires, a new pay off statement has to be requested.

J. THIRD PARTY LIENS

All third party liens attached to the subject property have to be accounted for. Liens from Home Owner Associations (HOA) or Condo Associations, Mechanics Liens, Tax Liens etc., have to be dealt with in order to get the short sale to its conclusion. The negotiators should be able to work out agreements acceptable to all parties. Usually third party lien holders are open to a negotiated settlement since normally it's a much better alternative to what they would receive after a foreclosure. This is not always the case with some types of liens, and it depends on the applicable laws (sometimes jurisdictional). It is recommended to consult an expert on the regulation at hand, and how to proceed.

K.   BUYER'S APPROVAL LETTER

If the prospective buyer will be financing part of the purchase, documentation showing his or her ability to obtain financing will be required. This is usually provided in the form of an approval letter issued by a mortgage lender on behalf of the buyer. This letter identifies the conditions under which such financing will be issued, and the terms. One of the things that will be looked at closely will be the amount of down payment that the buyer will bring to bear. It shows how committed they are to the purchase, and it improves the chances that a final approval will be issued. It also gives the purchaser more flexibility if the appraised value comes in lower than expected or if there is a counter offer by the mortgagee.

L.   CONTRACT OFFER

The contract offer already executed by the buyer(s) and the seller(s), and subject to the third party approval (the lender/mortgagee), is the key component to get the process started. These contracts that will be provided to the lender for consideration have to be structured for a short sale. Most jurisdictions have their standard "third party approval" addendums that will add that key feature to the contract offer. Sometimes, the lender will have their own addendums or other documentation that will also need to be signed by all the parties and included with the contract.

THE BANK PROCESS

The process to analyze and decision a short sale request varies from lender to lender, however the principal steps are very similar from one to the other.

First, the Loss Mitigation department will review the package to determine if all the required documentation has been submitted. Some departments will contact the home owner, or their designated representative if any of this documentation is missing. Unfortunately, some others will just turn down the request, or leave it on the side without working on it, because of the missing paperwork.

If the documentation is complete and acceptable, the case will be assigned to an analyst or case manager. This case manager will be the key person during the whole process. He or she will be making the recommendations, and help to dictate the terms under which the lender would accept the offer.

As previously mentioned, The Loss Mitigation Department / underwriter and the case manager will determine the merits of the case. They have to figure out if the short sale is the best solution for all parties, especially for the lender. In doing so, they will also try to determine if the current home owner is taking advantage of the situation or has a genuine and irreversible need to dispose of the property in this manner. The financial statement and other income and asset documentation will play an important role in this determination.

An appraisal or BPO will be ordered by the lender upon the successful completion of the initial part of the analysis. The purpose is to independently determine the current market value of the subject property on behalf of the mortgagee. They will contrast the findings to the offering price. This is a very important part of the process since this will help to determine if the offer is fair, and what will be the net loss to the lender if the offer is accepted. It also plays a role in whether the bank seeks a deficiency remedy against the mortgagor. There is a brief discussion on "deficiency judgments" ahead.

It is the general practice, that in the event that there are two loans on the subject property, and therefore two lenders with liens , that the short sale request be submitted to both lien holders for examination. The first lien holder has priority over the second lien holder, and in most cases a higher loan amount involved. The case manager of the first and the home owner (or the home owner's negotiator) will work with the second lien holder's case manager to coordinate the process and the decisions of both lien holders. The same process applies if there are more than two lien holders. The further out of first position the lien holder is, the less they will get back. In general, all lien holders have to be in agreement or the short sale will fail. However, most secondary lien holders agree to minimal amounts because if the property goes to foreclosure, the first lien holder will most likely get all the net funds and leave everybody else with very little or nothing at all. Some jurisdictions have exceptions to this practice, especially in the case of home owner associations. In addition, if there is any type of mortgage insurance or government loan guarantee, approval from that particular entity will most likely be required also. That process is usually handled by the lender's loss mitigation department, either thru direct endorsement or by coordinating with the related institution .

NEGOTIATING WITH THE BANK

Negotiating with the bank will be a case per case procedure, and one that will vary dramatically from lender to lender. Most of the time the lender will either outright accept the offer or reject it. This is the reason it is recommended that, to be most effective, the initial offer be priced in a way that will make sense to the lender. The Loss Mitigation Department will review the short sale offer and compare it to its other alternatives, such as foreclosure, and choose the one that will produce the best net, with the highest probabilities of success, in an acceptable time frame.

It is possible that the lender will counter the offer, and allow for negotiation. Other issues that could become negotiable are commissions and fees, timeframes, seller contributions, payment of past due homeowner association fees, taxes, and deficiencies. It is recommended to address all pertinent issues at the beginning as part of the initial package.

It is important to have all the most updated numbers and to do the math correctly. Past due fees, taxes, commissions and all other items including any third party fees have to be included in the calculations that bring about the net amount. One miscalculation could cause the deal to derail and possibly have to go back and start all over again. You could also find yourself at closing after all the hard work just to find out that the numbers are quite different than you had calculated. If the difference is big enough, it will most likely keep the closing from taking place. Being thorough is key.

WHAT TO EXPECT

Once all the documents are accepted by the bank the process will get started. Time frames will vary dramatically from one institution to another. The process, the criteria, and the results will vary from lender to lender and depending on the existing loan program on the property. Government backed loans such as FHA and VA will have slightly different criteria and processes than conventional loans. Jumbo and Portfolio loans will also differ somewhat, especially when looking at mortgagee criteria for accepting short sales. These last two types are less standardized than the previous categories, and therefore usually vary more depending on the lender and, or, investor. However these general guidelines apply to all loan types. Adapting to a specific situation will be necessary in some cases. Expect the process to last between 30 to 120 days as of the time of this writing. If it takes longer than that, it must have been stopped or seriously delayed at some point. In the near future, it is expected that procedures will be streamlined, and turn times will be cut shorter. Only time will tell. An emphasis needs to be placed on document tracking and following up with the assigned case manager. Making sure that the right person receives the right documentation is key. It is one of the main causes of delays and deal failure. At the very minimum, weekly contact with the case manager and his or her department is necessary to make sure they have what they need to complete their analysis of the case. Thorough follow up is essential for a successful and timely outcome.

As previously explained, the case manager will examine the financial documentation to form a picture of the homeowner's situation, and to help determine the actual need for the short sale. The contract will also be reviewed, as well as the purchaser's ability to acquire the property. The estimated settlement statement will help determine what the net outcome of the transaction will be for the bank. An appraisal or a BPO will be ordered by the case manager to see what the consensus of market value for the subject property is. This market study will be compared to the short sale offer. The loss mitigation department will use the documentation provided to help in these essential calculations. It is very important that the documentation provided is as accurate and current as possible. Otherwise, a decision might be made based on inaccurate or outdated information. Taxes due, association dues, legal fees, commissions, and other figures including third party fees, also have to be as accurate and current as possible. Otherwise they can derail the deal. For example, if the contract is based on a particular net proceed amount to the bank, and a particular fee was inaccurate, thus resulting in a substantially lower actual net proceed at closing, the bank could easily refuse to close, killing the deal at that point. If that happens, the process might have to start again from scratch and cause major delays, or worst, cause a buyer to cancel the

The Short Sale Handbook

contract altogether. This comment is repeated constantly thought the book because it is of upmost importance.

In the event that the bank approves the offer as submitted, it becomes a binding contract (since the third party approval has been granted within the time period agreed to). The bank will clearly stipulate the conditions under which is accepting the offer. One of them is the fees it will accept, and the minimum net it will accept. Again, a very important item to keep in mind. Another possible condition to watch out for is the request for the current owner to take an unsecured note for part or the whole deficiency amount or loss that the bank will suffer. These are becoming more uncommon but could be a factor when large losses will be incurred by the lender or a sizeable deal is being negotiated. In short, what this would mean is that the lender / mortgagee requires, as part of the deal, that the current borrower(s) repay a part or the whole amount the bank stands to lose under an unsecured loan, or possibly thru a loan secured by another property the individual might own.

WHAT IF THE BANK DENIES THE OFFER

If the mortgagee, or lender denies the offer being made on the short sale, the most likely reason will be a value related issue. If the market value indicated by the appraisal or BPO is substantially higher than the offer, then the lender will, in all likelihood, make a counter offer, or reject the deal altogether. The same could be said if the resulting net proceeds are unacceptable to the lender. This might be due to a combination of factors in relation to the price, such as the commissions, third party fees, or any other deductions that would result in a lower net than the lender is willing to accept. During the re-negotiations, these fees might have to be lowered, or completely eliminated in order to increase the net to the lender and reach the minimum proceed necessary to make the transaction possible.

A. INDICATION OF VALUE

Even if the lender rejects the offer completely, you might be able to determine what the offer amount, or net, the lender considers acceptable is. They might disclose it outright, or it might be implied by the net proceeds that they are expecting. This is critical since the current offer can be adjusted, or if that fails, a new offer can be made with a price that has a much more realistic chance of being approved by the lender.

Many times, there will be a difference of opinions about the value. Not always does the lender use the most qualified or reliable sources to determine their value. In other cases, there is simply a disagreement on market determinations. In very volatile markets, there will inevitably be inconsistent results and conflicts. If these conflicting value determinations cannot be resolved in order to reach a common ground, the deal will not be accomplished. Sometimes lenders will determine a value that is not consistent with the local market. Because of the bureaucracy involved, it might be impossible to find the agreement on value necessary to make the deal work. This is possibly the most difficult obstacle to overcome.

ACCEPTANCE OF THE SHORT SALE OFFER

If everything goes well and the lender accepts the short sale offer, closing will be expected shortly thereafter. As stated before, the lender will issue an acceptance letter announcing the terms under which it accepts the offer. Again, the items listed include, but are not limited, to minimum net proceeds to the lender, maximum commissions, length of time the acceptance is good for. It will indicate that there should be no cash allowed to go to the current owner, and whether the lender will seek to , or reserve the right to collect the deficiency from the mortgagor(s). If they are not seeking to collect, the letter should also include a clause that specifically states that the mortgagee will not seek a deficiency remedy against the owner and / or mortgagor for the shortage.

A.   WATCH OUT FOR: REQUIREMENT FOR A PROMISORY NOTE

Again, as a condition to the acceptance of the short sale offer, the lender might request that the current owner(s) / mortgagor(s) sign a secured, or unsecured note promising to pay the amount that the lender is losing if it goes thru with the short sale. This is a very important consideration for all debtors. By accepting this stipulation, the current mortgagor is taking on the responsibility of paying back this sum without possessing the underlying asset that it was originally secured with. It should be a priority during the short sale negotiations, to get the lender to agree not to impose this requirement as part of their acceptance of the offer.

B.   WATCH OUT FOR: DEFICIENCY JUDGEMENT

It can't be overstated how important it is to obtain a guarantee in writing from the lender, as part of their acceptance, that they will not seek a deficiency judgment against the current owner. As mentioned before, a deficiency judgment will obligate the current mortgagor to pay the difference between the actual balance and the net proceeds. This will most likely be done thru the court system, where the lender (mortgagee) will seek to obtain the judgment against the mortgagor. It is in the best interest of the current owner / mortgagor to obtain the guarantee from the lender, in writing, stating they will not seek such judgment or collection. If applicable, in jurisdictions that follow the process of judicial foreclosure, a dismissal "with prejudice" should be sought by the mortgagor(s).

THE CLOSING

The day of settlement, the closing agent will put together all the figures, and if there is buyer financing involved, will handle that part too. We repeat, it is important that the numbers are added up correctly, with the most up to date data. Information such as unpaid taxes, association or condo fees due, any applicable third party fees etc., need to be accurate and properly documented. Unpleasant surprises can derail the closing on a short sale very quickly. The lender expects to get no less than the agreed upon net proceed. Anything lower can lead to a failed closing. It is very important that all information is obtained early enough in the process to avoid miscalculations.

It is also important that the buyer's financing, if applicable, is done in a timely fashion. The lender has issued a time frame by which the closing has to be carried out. Violating this deadline can be disastrous for the process. Contract deadlines also have to be extended if they are due to expire before closing.

The lien holders will review all the figures and give their respective approval to close if the numbers are acceptable as per the agreement. Once the closing is completed, the old mortgagor(s) is released from his or her obligations (as long as there are no deficiency provisions), and transfers possession of the property to the new owner(s) free of liens.

PRECAUTIONS

As previously stated, short sales are generally considered the best alternative to obtain relief for home owners that are underwater, or upside down, and unable to continue to make payments on their properties. However, there are possible ramifications and consequences stemming from a short sale that have to be taken into account.

A. AGAIN: DEFICIENCY JUDGEMENTS

It cannot be emphasized enough that deficiency arrangements that keeps the mortgagor / owner on the hook for the current mortgage have to be avoided as much as possible. It is of great importance that the lender's acceptance letter indicates that no deficiency judgments or any other arrangement that require substantial monetary remedies from the current home owner will be sought by the lender. It should make it clear that the mortgagor is completely free of any further financial obligations for subject transaction. It is good to know that some jurisdictions do not allow for the lender(s) to seek deficiency judgments if they agree to the short sale, thus making it even more advantageous for the mortgagor(s). Also, some legal opinions suggest that by releasing the lien on the property, approving the short sale, and issuing certain forms of 1099's to the mortgagor(s), the lender(s) are in fact agreeing to settle the debt completely for less than was owed, thus precluding them from seeking additional remedies from the mortgagor(s). This view has not been validated by the court systems in general at this point.

B. POSSIBLE TAX CONSEQUENCES

A tax advisor should be consulted prior to executing a short sale. It is very likely that there might be tax consequences to be dealt with from the short sale after its completion. It is possible that the current mortgagor can be held liable for taxes from a short sale. At first this might be viewed as counterintuitive since the owner as well as the lender is taking a loss on the transaction. However, the portion of the debt that is "forgiven" by the lender can become taxable. The mortgagor will very likely receive a 1099 equivalent to the amount forgiven (the deficiency). An analysis of how this possibility could affect the transaction itself, and the overall tax profile for the individual home owner should be thoroughly considered before making the initial decision on pursuing a short sale.

Please review IRS Publication 4681 and news release IR-2008-17 . As of the time of this writing they contain the most current IRS guidelines on the subject.

C. CREDIT CONSEQUENCES

Credit consequences stemming from a short sale should also be considered before thinking about a short sale solution. In many cases the home owner will be behind on the mortgage payments and the credit is already impacted, probably severely. Although a short sale is widely considered to have less of a harmful effect on credit ratings than a foreclosure, it will still bear a heavy toll on the individual's credit. There is also a difference between the effect of a short sale where the mortgage is delinquent before the short sale is executed, and one where the mortgage payments have been current up until the day of the short sale. According to current agency guidelines, a non-delinquent short sale will be looked at in a better light than one that had been delinquent prior to the short sale. However, opinions vary as to how a lender's loss mitigation department will look at a short sale offer where the underlying mortgage is non-delinquent.

D. EFFECT OF A SHORT SALE REQUEST ON THE FORECLOSURE PROCESS

If the lender holding the mortgage on the subject property has already started a foreclosure process before the short sale petition is made, or during the time the short sale is being processed, a formal request to stop the foreclosure process from moving forward must be made. In most jurisdictions, the lender / mortgagee is not required by law to stop the foreclosure process because of a short sale request. Most lenders will allow time for the submission to be reviewed. However, sometimes due to internal bureaucracy, or simply because different departments handle each process, the foreclosure keeps moving forward. It is very important that the foreclosure postponement or cancellation is confirmed with both the lender and the entity engaged in the actual execution of the foreclosure sale. This entity could be a trustee or a law firm that usually handles such matters. Some states and jurisdictions have instituted mediation requirements, or similar programs, that mandate lenders to meet with the home owner, mortgagor, and an appointed mediator, to explore available options before the foreclosure becomes imminent. This would be a good opportunity to bring up the fact that a short sale is being sought, and to request the postponement or cancellation of the foreclosure in order to give enough time to the parties to bring the short sale to a successful conclusion. Short sales usually take a significant amount of time to process and close. They also have enough of a failure rate, specially the first time around, that needs to be accounted for. It is highly recommended that the process get started with enough time to avoid becoming involved in a foreclosure action while trying to short- sell the property. Not only does this increase the stress levels significantly for everyone, but sometimes, the property gets foreclosed while the short sale is still being reviewed. Better preparation and anticipation would significantly reduce the probability of this occurrence. This situation must be avoided if at all possible.

USING A PROFESSIONAL

In most cases it is highly recommended that the home owner obtain the services of professionals to assist in the cumbersome short sale process and it's repercussions . All the numerous steps that need to be achieved could be overwhelming for the home owner(s) to do by themselves. There is also the very important fact that a team of proven, experienced, and highly effective professionals will substantially increase the probability of success. In most cases well worth the expense. At a minimum, the team should consist of an experienced real estate agent, well versed in short sales, and an experienced, effective (high success rate) negotiator. There are many companies and individuals advertising services for the negotiation of short sales and other remedies for home owners in trouble. Like in any other business, there are some good ones, and many bad ones. This is also a field that has attracted a lot of scam artists. Be careful of who you work with. In my experience, working with a competent attorney that specializes in short sale negotiations, and processes, has always brought the best results. It also eliminates in large part, the possibility of being taken advantage of, or falling in with someone who is negligent with their customer's cases. Attorneys have the advantage of being able to deal with any legal issues that might arise, where only someone with a law license can be of use. They can also give competent legal advice on the process and its ramifications. A good title company that can deal with the additional demands of a short sale is also recommended. Sometimes the title company and the attorney work within the same firm. This is not unusual and can be advantageous. Last, but not least, and as mentioned previously, it is advisable to consult an accountant or CPA before, during, and after the process of the short sale. It is very important to know what the tax, and personal financial consequences of a short sale are before the start, and what the effects are if there are any changes in the disposition of the short sale outcome.

SUMMARY

It is evident at this time that we are going thru the worst housing crisis since the Great Depression. In some ways, the scope and dimensions are much bigger today than back then. The net equity loss of our residential housing market runs into the trillions of dollars. The loss of wealth is immeasurable across the country. In addition, the unemployment / underemployment rate, lack of credit, equity market fluctuations, and overall weak economy have compounded the problem into what can be considered a perfect storm. As a result, an ever increasing percentage of home owners are in the very difficult position of owning properties that they can no longer afford to maintain, and that at the same time have values that leave them no way out under customary circumstances. The exit strategies available at this point are painful no matter how you look at them. The short sale has become the best option for these individuals. If done correctly, the short sale can alleviate an unbearable financial situation for these home owners, and allow them to move on with their lives with the least amount of damage. It also allows for lenders to recover a significant amount of their investment and help to end this banking and housing crisis, as well as provide countless new home buyers with opportunities they could only dream of before.

SUBMISSION CHECK LIST

_____ Cover letter

_____ Authorization Form (If a third party)

_____ Estimated Settlement Statement / Net Sheet

_____ Hardship letter

_____ Financial Statement

_____ Profit and Loss Statement

_____ Tax returns

_____ Supporting Documentation

_____ Payoff Statement(s)

_____ Third Party Liens

_____ Buyer's approval letter (if financing is being used)

_____ Listing Agreement (if using a real estate agent)

_____ Contract Offer

DOCUMENT CHECKLIST

_____ Mortgage Statements

_____ Contact information for all parties

_____ Financial Forms

_____ Pay Stubs (One month's worth)

_____ Last two years tax returns (extension if not filed)

_____ Last two years W2s (if employed)

_____ Last two years corporate taxes (if applicable)

_____ Profit and Loss Statement YTD (if self employed)

_____ Form 4506 or 4506 T (If required)

_____ Two consecutive months of bank statements (all liquid assets)

_____ Homestead documentation (if applicable)

_____ Social Security , pension income documentation (if applicable)

_____ Divorce Decree (if applicable)

_____ Bankruptcy documentation (if applicable)

_____ Miscellaneous (if applicable)

_____ Comparables (if required)

APPENDIX A: EXHIBITS

Chase Home Finance LLC
9200 Oakdale Avenue
Chatsworth, CA 91311
800-848-9380

<table>
<tr><td></td><td>Approval letter with
Deficiency Waiver
for a First Trust</td></tr>
</table>

RE: Loan: ▮▮▮▮▮▮
      Borrower(s): ▮▮▮▮▮▮   Buyer(s): ▮▮▮▮▮▮▮▮▮▮▮

      Property Address:
      ▮▮▮▮▮▮▮▮▮▮
      ▮▮▮▮▮▮

To Whom It May Concern:

This letter will confirm Chase Home Finance LLC's (Chase) approval of the sales contract pertaining to the above referenced property for $780,000 between the above parties. *Please be advised this is not the final approval for the referenced sale.* Once the HUD-1 is approved, closing instructions will be issued and the closing may occur. *The property must be lien free at the time of closing.* It is our understanding that the following are the expenses to the seller:

Actual proceeds (sales price) $780,000
Seller's closing costs

     Broker Commission $31,200
     Sellers Closing Costs $20,914.04
     Seller Contribution: $0

Total Proceeds to be received by Chase: $727,885.96

The amount paid to Chase is for the release of Chase's security interest(s), and we will waive the remaining deficiency balance on the account, totaling $296,903.99.

The Borrower's costs and contributions are estimates provided by the Escrow Company. Chase, under no circumstances will accept less than the approximate net amount stated and may require additional funds if actual costs are less than those provided by the Escrow Company.

It is our understanding that escrow will close on or before as this approval is based on figures good through this date, Chase must be advised if there is a postponement of the closing. Additionally, should any variances occur in the approved transaction, Chase must be contacted to approve the changes. Chase is under no obligation to approve the changes and may require the revision of submitted changes.

If Chase does not approve changes, Chase may rescind its approval of the sale. **If we approve an extension of the closing date per diem interest may be assessed.**
Further requirements of this approval are as follows:

1. Any required borrower contributions ($0) are to be paid at closing regardless of net from the sale.
Chase shall not accept less than the stated net amount. Borrower shall be responsible for any additional costs, which may cause the true net amount to be less than the net amount stated.

2. The borrower (seller) must net zero. All proceeds are to be remitted to the lender. All amounts remaining and retained by borrower shall automatically be assigned to lender even if proceeds exceed the approved net amount. **Neither the borrower nor any other party may receive any sales proceeds or any other funds as a result of this transaction**. The borrower must assign to Chase any rights to escrow funds, insurance proceeds, or refunds from prepaid expenses. Chase can apply the proceeds of the sale to the outstanding indebtedness in any manner that Chase should elect.

3. The final proposed HUD-1 settlement statement shall be faxed to Chase for final approval no later than 72 hours before the closing date (excluding weekends and holidays) or Chase may rescind its approval of the sale. Once the closing statement is received and approved, closing instructions will be sent to the closer.

4. All pro-rations are to be figured to the date of closing and are considered final. Tax pro-rations are to be based on not more than 100% of actual tax.

5. Please overnight to the address below. Please note new mailing address:

Documents to:	Funds to:
Chase Home Finance	Chase Home Finance
Attn: ███████████	Attn: Short Sale Department
Mailstop: CA2-4304	Mailstop: OH4-7133
9200 Oakdale Ave, Floor 1	3415 Vision Drive
Chatsworth, CA 91311	Columbus, OH 43219

If the final closing instructions are not followed in their entirety, the lien will not be satisfied and the proceeds check will be returned.

Sincerely,

███████████

Loss Mitigation Short Sales
Chase Home Finance LLC
Phone: 800-700-0043
Fax # 302-669-2220

GMAC Mortgage

3451 Hammond Ave
P.O. Box 780
Waterloo, IA 50704-0780

RE: Account Number: ███████████
     Property Address: ███████████████████████
                        ████████   ████████

Dear Borrower(s):

GMAC Mortgage. LLC would like to provide you with the opportunity to settle your loan for less than the total amount currently required to payoff your loan in full. In consideration for the amount of $6000.00 GMAC Mortgage, LLC will forgive any remaining amounts due and, where our lien remains on your property, will take the necessary steps to release that lien. In order to accept this offer, this amount must be received in our office, via certified funds, no later than ████████

Please overnight certified funds to: or, Wire funds to
GMAC Mortgage. LLC   JP Morgan Chase Bank, NA
3451 Hammond Avenue   For GMAC Mortgage, LLC
Waterloo, IA 50702   ABA Routing Number: ████████
Attention: Cashiering Department   Account Number: ████████
                                            Mortgage Number: ████████
                                            Customer Name: ████████████

Please note that because the amount we are willing to accept is less than the total amount due to pay your loan in full. the account will be reported to the credit bureaus as "settled for less than amount owed." This may have a negative impact on your credit. In addition, this transaction may have tax consequences; therefore, we urge you seek advice from a tax professional in order to determine to what extent any such consequences may impact you.

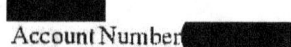

Account Number ███████████

If you have any questions, please contact us at 800-850-4622 ext.7348543 Mon -Fri 8am to 5pm Eastern time.

Sincerely,

Recovery Department
Loan Servicing

Notice: Federal law requires that we advise you that this notice is from a debt collector attempting to collect on a debt and any information obtained will be used for that purpose.

If you are currently involved in a bankruptcy proceeding or have been discharged of your personal liability for the repayment of this debt, this notice is being provided for informational purposes only, it is not an attempt to hold you personally responsible for the debt and applies only to the lien on your property and not to you personally

5:42

PRE-APPROVED PROPERTY SALE

Nationstar
MORTGAGE
f/k/a
Centex Home Equity Company, LLC
350 Highland Dr.
Lewisville, TX 75067
Attn: Foreclosure Prevention

RE: Loan #: ▓▓▓▓▓
        Property Address:
▓▓▓▓▓▓▓▓▓

Approval for a First Trust WITH promissory note requirement

        Borrower (s): ▓▓▓▓

Nationstar Mortgage LLC f/k/a Centex Home Equity Company, LLC ("Nationstar Mortgage") approves the sale of the property contingent upon the following:

Net proceeds to Nationstar Mortgage:	Not less than $294,309.98
Funds from impound (if any):	To be applied to the deficiency
Payment date:	▓▓▓▓▓

Nationstar Mortgage agrees (1) file a withdrawal of the Notice, and (2) provide any documents necessary for release after we receive the funds and (3) waive any remaining deficiency balance in consideration for all borrowers executing the attached Promissory Note. NO FUNDS ARE TO BE RELEASED TO THE BORROWER.

The attached Promissory Note in the amount of ▓▓▓ will need to be executed. The original signed Promissory Note must be forwarded with the net proceeds along with a copy of the final settlement statement.

The following closing costs should not exceed the given amount:

Commissions	$19,800.00
Negotiated 2nd Lien Release	$5,000.00
Total closing costs	$12,624.26
Cash from Seller	$500.00
Extension Fee	$1,234.24

Payment will only be accepted by *certified funds* for the entire amount listed above to the appropriate address listed below. In the event that we do not receive the entire amount due, in immediately available funds, on or before ▓▓▓▓▓▓ 12 noon (CST), this pre - approved property sale offer will terminate and be of no force and effect. Please fax an executed final settlement statement & wire confirmation to 972.459.6273. **Please be advised that if a foreclosure sale is pending, the foreclosure sale date will not be postponed to allow this short sale closing.**

Regards,

Foreclosure Prevention Manager
▓▓▓▓▓▓▓

PAYOFF FUNDS MUST BE REMITTED USING CERTIFIED FUNDS OR BY WIRE TRANSFER ONLY. If using wire transfer, forward to: JP Morgan Chase, Routing ▓▓▓▓▓, for credit to Nationstar Mortgage Payment Clearing Account ▓▓▓▓▓ If mailing certified funds, make payable to Nationstar Mortgage LLC and forward to the address listed at the top of page. Funds received after 3:00pm Central Time may be posted on the following business day. Please include the Mortgagor's Loan Number on all correspondence. **Loan number and Borrower name must be attached to wire.** Note: All short sales of loans that have mortgage insurance coverage are subject to mortgage insurer approval.

IMPORTANT NOTICE

We reserve the right to adjust any portion of this statement at any time for one or more of the following reasons, but not limited to: recent advances, returned items, additional fees or charges, disbursements made on your behalf, scheduled payment(s) from an escrow account, transfer of servicing and/or inadvertent clerical errors.

This payoff estimate does not waive our rights to collect any funds which become due on this account as a result of any subsequent adjustments. Additionally, Nationstar Mortgage LLC will not provide reconveyance or release of the Security Instrument until the net proceeds and all other items required above have been received.

WELLS FARGO

Wells Fargo Services
MAC N9777-113-HEQ
PO BOX 5169
Sioux Falls, SD 57117-5169

Approval for a
Second Trust
settled in full for
less than the
balance due, and
no deficiency

Re: Account Number: ███████████████

Dear ████████████████████

This letter confirms that with your remittance of $90,000.00 on ███████████, Wells Fargo considers the above-referenced Account to be settled in full, for less than the full balance. In consideration of this settlement, Wells Fargo will cease further collection efforts and the remaining balance will be charged-off.

Wells Fargo will report the Account to the credit bureau reporting agencies to which it reports as a charged-off account that was paid in full for less than the full balance.

Please be advised that the Internal Revenue Service (IRS) requires financial institutions to annually report to the IRS discharges of indebtedness. In the event a settlement of this account results in a forgiveness of $600 or more of the principle balance due on the account, we may be required to file an informational return with the IRS reporting the forgiven amount. Please contact your tax advisor with any questions about how this may affect your income tax liability.

If you have any questions, please call me at 1-800-944-4601 Monday through Thursday 8 a.m. to 9 p.m. CT, Friday 8 a.m. to 5 p.m. CT, Saturday 8 a.m. to 12 p.m. CT. If I am unavailable, any representative can assist you.

Sincerely,

EM
Home Equity Collections Servicing

HEQSIF01.doc

SUNTRUST™

Approval letter for a second trust with no debt forgiveness and no deficiency waiver

SunTrust Bank, Inc.
1001 Semmes Ave. RVW-3054
Richmond, VA 23224
Tel 888.886.0696
Fax 804.674.0507

Name: ▓▓▓▓
Address: ▓▓▓▓▓▓
City, State: ▓▓▓▓▓▓

RE: Mortgage Loan Acct # ▓▓▓▓
Property address: ▓▓▓▓▓▓

Dear ▓▓▓▓

SunTrust Bank is offering you the following settlement on mortgage account in the form of this short sale agreement. *This offer is good thru* ▓▓▓▓. If the preliminary terms of this settlement offer are not met (i.e. either this short sale agreement is not signed and returned, or the property is not sold during the period of time specified above), this offer of settlement shall be withdrawn, the lien will not be released, and you will be required to pay the full balance outstanding on your SunTrust Bank as of the date of this letter and noted herein.

Upon receipt of certified funds or a check drawn on the account of the closing attorney or settlement agent, of not less than *$5,000.00* on or before ▓▓▓▓, and confirmation, via a copy of the HUD-1 Settlement Statement that you received absolutely no proceeds from this sale, it is agreed that SunTrust Bank will release its lien encumbering your property, but will not release your obligation on the underlying personal debt unless you make satisfactory arrangements with SunTrust to satisfy all or part of your Loan or Line Agreement.

Outlined below is a detailed accounting of the proposed distribution of the sales proceeds, and Net Proceeds payable to SunTrust, which SunTrust has agreed are acceptable:

Actual Sales Price		$330,000.00
Cash Contribution		$0.00
Realtor(s) Commission	(	$19,800.00)
Seller Closing Costs – Not to Exceed	(	$12,793.13)
Buyer Closing Costs – Not to Exceed	(	$0.00)
Allowance to subordinate/superior liens(s) if applicable	(	$292,406.87)
Net Proceeds payable to SunTrust		$5,000.00

SunTrust Bank must be in receipt of the *final* HUD1 Settlement Statement, no later than forty-eight (48) hours prior to the actual closing date for approval. Please email to ▓▓▓▓

To expedite lien release processing, send the certified funds to:
SunTrust Bank, Inc.
Attention: ▓▓▓▓
1001 Semmes Ave. RVW-3054
Richmond, VA 23224

FUNDS RECEIVED WITHOUT A COPY OF THE EXECUTED HUD, AND THE EXECUTED APPROVAL LETTER, WILL BE RETURNED WITHIN 24 HOURS.

OMB NO. 2502-0265

A.	B. TYPE OF LOAN:
U.S. DEPARTMENT OF HOUSING & URBAN DEVELOPMENT **SETTLEMENT STATEMENT**	1. ☐ FHA 2. ☐ FmHA 3. ☐ CONV. UNINS. 4. ☐ VA 5. ☐ CONV. INS.
	6. FILE NUMBER: ▓▓
	7. LOAN NUMBER:
	8. MORTGAGE INS CASE NUMBER:

C. NOTE: *This form is furnished to give you a statement of actual settlement costs. Amounts paid to and by the settlement agent are shown. Items marked "[POC]" were paid outside the closing; they are shown here for informational purposes and are not included in the totals.*

1.0 3/98 (11-3126.PFD/11-3126/37)

D. NAME AND ADDRESS OF BORROWER:	E. NAME AND ADDRESS OF SELLER:	F. NAME AND ADDRESS OF LENDER: CASH ← Cash Sale

G. PROPERTY LOCATION:	H. SETTLEMENT AGENT:	I. SETTLEMENT DATE:
	PLACE OF SETTLEMENT	

J. SUMMARY OF BORROWER'S TRANSACTION		K. SUMMARY OF SELLER'S TRANSACTION	
100. GROSS AMOUNT DUE FROM BORROWER:		**400. GROSS AMOUNT DUE TO SELLER:**	
101. Contract Sales Price	180,000.00	401. Contract Sales Price	180,000.00
102. Personal Property		402. Personal Property	
103. Settlement Charges to Borrower (Line 1400)	20,166.55	403.	
104.		404.	
105.		405.	
Adjustments For Items Paid By Seller in advance		*Adjustments For Items Paid By Seller in advance*	
106. City/Town Taxes to		406. City/Town Taxes to	
107. County Taxes to		407. County Taxes to	
108. Assessments to		408. Assessments to	
109. HOA DUES ▓▓	4.16	409. HOA DUES ▓▓	4.16
110. Association Dues ▓▓	11.20	410. Association Dues ▓▓	11.20
111.		411.	
112.		412.	
120. GROSS AMOUNT DUE FROM BORROWER	200,181.91	**420. GROSS AMOUNT DUE TO SELLER**	180,015.36
200. AMOUNTS PAID BY OR IN BEHALF OF BORROWER:		**500. REDUCTIONS IN AMOUNT DUE TO SELLER:**	
201. Deposit or earnest money	5,000.00	501. Excess Deposit (See Instructions)	
202. Principal Amount of New Loan(s)		502. Settlement Charges to Seller (Line 1400)	12,391.81
203. Existing loan(s) taken subject to		503. Existing loan(s) taken subject to	
204.		504. Payoff First Mortgage to CHASE	156,346.22
205.		505. Payoff Second Mortgage to GMAC	4,000.00
206.		506.	
207.		507. PER DIEM to CHASE	377.30
208.		508.	
209.		509.	
Adjustments For Items Unpaid By Seller		*Adjustments For Items Unpaid By Seller*	
210. City/Town Taxes to		510. City/Town Taxes to	
211. County Taxes ▓▓	1,653.47	511. County Taxes ▓▓	1,653.47
212. Assessments to		512. Assessments to	
213.		513.	
214.		514.	
215.		515.	
216.		516.	
217.		517. Delinquent HOA ▓▓	5,246.56
218.	·	518. 2010 Property Tax to ▓▓ County/POC$3862.51	
219.		519.	
220. TOTAL PAID BY/FOR BORROWER	6,653.47	**520. TOTAL REDUCTION AMOUNT DUE SELLER**	180,015.36
300. CASH AT SETTLEMENT FROM/TO BORROWER:		**600. CASH AT SETTLEMENT TO/FROM SELLER:**	
301. Gross Amount Due From Borrower (Line 120)	200,181.91	601. Gross Amount Due To Seller (Line 420)	180,015.36
302. Less Amount Paid By/For Borrower (Line 220)	(6,653.47)	602. Less Reductions Due Seller (Line 520)	(180,015.36)
303. CASH (X FROM) (TO) BORROWER	193,528.44	603. CASH (TO) (FROM) SELLER	0.00

No funds go to the seller

Page 2

L. SETTLEMENT CHARGES

	PAID FROM BORROWER'S FUNDS AT SETTLEMENT	PAID FROM SELLER'S FUNDS AT SETTLEMENT
700. TOTAL COMMISSION Based on Price $ 180,000.00 @ 5.0000 % 9,000.00		
Division of Commission (line 700) as Follows:		
701. $ 4,500.00 to ███		
702. $ 4,500.00 to ███		
703. Commission Paid at Settlement		9,000.00
704. Transaction/Processing Fee to ███	495.00	
800. ITEMS PAYABLE IN CONNECTION WITH LOAN		
801. Loan Origination Fee % to		
802. Loan Discount % to		
803. Appraisal Fee to		
804. Credit Report to		
805. Lender's Inspection Fee to		
806. Mortgage Ins. App. Fee to		
807. Assumption Fee to		
808.		
809.		
810.		
811.		
900. ITEMS REQUIRED BY LENDER TO BE PAID IN ADVANCE		
901. Interest From to @ $ /day (days %)		
902. MIP TotIns. for LifeOfLoan for months to		
903. Hazard Insurance Premium for 1.0 years to		
904.		
905.		
1000. RESERVES DEPOSITED WITH LENDER		
1001. Hazard Insurance months @ $ per month		
1002. Mortgage Insurance months @ $ per month		
1003. City/Town Taxes months @ $ per month		
1004. County Taxes months @ $ per month		
1005. Assessments months @ $ per month		
1006. months @ $ per month		
1007. months @ $ per month		
1008. Aggregate Adjustment months @ $ per month		
1100. TITLE CHARGES		
1101. Settlement or Closing Fee to ███	595.00	836.81
1102. Abstract or Title Search to ███ Title Insurance Company		150.00
1103. Title Examination to		
1104. Title Insurance Binder to		
1105. Copy/Fax/Wire/Warehousing to		
1106. Postage/ Shipping & Handling to		
1107. Attorney's Fees to		
(includes above item numbers:)		
1108. Title Insurance to ███		975.00
(includes above item numbers:)		
1109. Lender's Coverage $ $25 Risk		
1110. Owner's Coverage $ 180,000.00 975.00 Promulgated		
1111.		
1112.		
1113.		
1200. GOVERNMENT RECORDING AND TRANSFER CHARGES		
1201. Recording Fees: Deed $ 27.00 ; Mortgage $; Releases $	27.00	
1202. City/County Tax/Stamps: Deed ; Mortgage		
1203. State Tax/Starrps: 1,080.00 ; Mortgage		1,080.00
1204. Intangible Tax Board of County Commissioners		
1205.		
1300. ADDITIONAL SETTLEMENT CHARGES		
1301. Survey to ███		
1302. Pest Inspection to		
1303. Lien Search to ███		175.00
1304. Association Estoppel to ███		175.00
1305. See addit'l disb. exhibit to ███	19,049.55	
1400. TOTAL SETTLEMENT CHARGES (Enter on Lines 103, Section J and 502, Section K)	20,166.55	12,391.81

Certified to be a true copy.
* - Indicates seller paid these closing costs for the buyer, if applicable, per the agreed contractual amount.

(11-3128 / 11-3128 / 37)

Borrower(s): ██████████████

Seller(s): ██████████████

Lender: CASH

Settlement Agent: ████████████████

Place of Settlement ██████████████████

Settlement Date: ████████

Property Location: ████████████████

Third party liens such as an HOA can be negotiated between the parties

Additional Adjustments For Items Paid By Seller In Advance (Borrower Debit)

Description	Amount	From/Through	Prorated Amount
HOA DUES	128.93	██████████████	4.16
		Total Line 109/409	4.16
Association Dues	347.13	██████████████	11.20
		Total Line 110/410	11.20

Additional Disbursements

Payee/Description	Note/Ref No.	Borrower	Seller
GMAC Contribution to 2nd lien		2,000.00	
███████████ Contirubtion to HOA Master		4,729.12	
███████████ Contribution to HOA ████		11,754.37	
████████ HOA DUES	JUNE	128.93	
██████████ HOA DUES	JUNE	437.13	
Total Additional Disbursements shown on Line 1305		$ 19,049.55	$ 0.00

Seller Loan Payoff Details

Payoff First Mortgage   to CHASE

Loan Payoff	As of		
Total Additional Interest		days @	Per Diem
Total Loan Payoff	156,346.22		

Payoff Second Mortgage   to GMAC

Loan Payoff	As of		
Total Additional Interest		days @	Per Diem
Total Loan Payoff	4,000.00		

I have carefully reviewed the HUD-1 Settlement Statement and to the best of my knowledge and belief, it is a true and accurate statement of all receipts and disbursements made on my account or by me in this transaction. I further certify that I have received a copy of the HUD-1 Settlement Statement.

████████████████   ████████████████

(11-3128.PFD/11-3128/37)

BY: _____
    President

To the best of my knowledge, the HUD-1 Settlement Statement which I have prepared is a true and accurate account of the funds which were received and have been or will be disbursed by the undersigned as part of the settlement of this transaction.

_____

▓▓▓▓▓▓▓▓▓▓▓▓▓
Settlement Agent

(11-3128.PFD/11-3128/37)

In order for us to evaluate your Short Sale request, you must complete this packet, sign in all the required places and fax or mail it to Chase with the required documentation.

Please keep a copy of everything you send to us for your records.

This packet contains the following:

INFORMATION ONLY

1. Required Documentation Checklist –
Detailed list of the documents you must send to us in addition to the packet
   a. From You, the Borrower and Co-borrower
   b. From Your Real Estate Agent

2. Authorization to Provide and Release Information –
Grants Chase permission to provide information pertaining to your mortgage to necessary agents

3. Request for Consideration of Short Sale –
Information about your property, loans, income, etc., as well as details on the circumstances that have made it difficult for you to stay up-to-date with your mortgage payments

4. IRS Form 4506-T Request for Transcript of Tax Return –
Allows Chase to receive a transcript of your tax return to verify income information

5. Dodd-Frank Certification –
The federal government now requires that all borrowers seeking assistance under the Making Home Affordable (MHA) Program complete and sign the enclosed Dodd-Frank Certification

If you need any assistance completing this packet please contact us at 866-233-5320.

Please send the completed packet as well as all required documentation:

BY REGULAR MAIL:	BY OVERNIGHT MAIL:	BY FAX:
Chase Fulfillment Center P.O. Box 469030 Glendale, CO 80246	Chase Fulfillment Center 710 South Ash St. Suite #200 Glendale, CO 80246	866-220-4130

Chase and FedEx Office are offering you an easy way to return your loan documents. You can find the nearest FedEx Office location offering this service by visiting www.fedex.com/us/office, entering your ZIP code in the *Find a FedEx Location* box and selecting *FedEx Kinko's is now FedEx Office*. Bring your documents to one of these select FedEx Office locations and tell them you are returning these documents to Chase. Provide your name, ZIP code, and phone number to the counter agent, and they will ship your documents to us at no charge. For more information go to www.chase.com/fedex.

↑
Free shipping
courtesy of Chase

Important Information

Loan Number: _____

1A. FROM YOU, THE BORROWER AND CO-BORROWER

If you are a Wage Earner (you receive a W-2 from your employer) please provide:

☐ Two (2) most recent Pay Stubs (two for each borrower)

☐ Length of service with Current Employer: Borrower Year(s):_____ Month(s):_____   Co-borrower Year(s):_____ Month(s):_____

☐ Most recent one (1) month's complete Bank Statement

If you are Self Employed, please provide:

☐ P & L Statement / Audited or reviewed YTD Income Statement (must provide)

☐ Most recent two (2) years' Tax Returns completed (personal and business, signed with all pages) or 1099s or most recent two (2) years filed and proof of extension

☐ Last four (4) months complete Business and Personal Bank Statements (must provide all pages. If a business account is not used, provide a written statement stating a business account is not used)

Everyone must provide the following:

☐ Most recent statement(s) supporting assets listed on page 2 of the Request for Consideration of Short Sale Form (must provide all pages of statements)

☐ Most recent completed Tax Return (signed with all pages) or most recent filed and proof of extension (signed with all pages)

☐ Proof of occupancy (if owner occupied) – a recent utility bill in your name at property address

☐ If loan is Non-Escrowed:

   A) Copy of the most recent property tax bill(s) with a copy of the cancelled check for all applicable taxes (County, City, School, etc.)

   B) Copy of the current insurance declaration page for all applicable coverage types (must show premium amount for homeowner's, flood, and wind)

   C) Proof of payment of Homeowner's Association Fees (if applicable)

INFORMATION ONLY

☐ If Non-Owner Occupied:

   A) Rental Income with copies of Rental Agreement if a tenant resides in the property

   B) Amount of Principal, Interest, Taxes, Insurance, and Home Owner Dues for Primary Residence

   C) Primary Residence Address

☐ Authorization to Provide and Release Information – Allows Realtor or designee to discuss the account with Chase, if desired. **Be sure to sign this form**

☐ Completed Request for Consideration of Short Sale Form (enclosed). **Be sure to sign and date this form.**

☐ Completed 4506-T – Request for Transcript of Tax Return (enclosed.) **Be sure to sign and date this form.**

1B. FROM YOUR REAL ESTATE AGENT

☐ Listing Agreement

☐ Detailed Listing History (MLS Printout)

☐ Sales / Purchase Contract (Signed Offer)

☐ 3 Comparable Active Listings/3 Comparable Sales/Pictures of the Property & Neighborhood

☐ HUD (Estimated Closing Statement)

These forms are for informational purpose. Please obtain the most updated forms and information by contacting the appropriate lender or visiting their website for instructions.

Loan Number: _____

INFORMATION ONLY

TO: Chase

DATE: _____

BORROWER(S):   _____

PROPERTY ADDRESS: _____

_____

I/(We), _____(borrower(s) name(s)) , currently residing

at _____ in the County of _____,

State of _____, hereby authorize Chase/JPMorgan Chase Bank, N.A (collectively "Chase") to release, furnish, and provide any

information related to my mortgage under loan number _____ to:

Company Name: _____

Company Phone Number: _____

Fax Number: _____

**I UNDERSTAND THAT THIS AUTHORIZATION IS VALID UNTIL SUCH TIME
THAT CHASE CONFIRMS IT HAS RECEIVED WRITTEN NOTICE FROM ME
REVOKING THIS PRIOR AGREEMENT.**

_____   _____
Borrower Signature   Co-borrower Signature

_____   _____
Borrower Name (Printed)   Co-borrower Name (Printed)

These forms are for informational purpose. Please obtain the most updated forms and information
by contacting the appropriate lender or visiting their website for instructions.

REQUEST FOR CONSIDERATION OF SHORT SALE FORM

CHASE

Servicer: _____   Loan Number: _____

BORROWER	CO-BORROWER

BORROWER

Borrower's name

Social Security number   Date of Birth

Home phone number with area code

Cell or work number with area code

CO-BORROWER

Co-borrower's name

Social Security number   Date of Birth

Home phone number with area code

Cell or work number with area code

I want to: ☐ Keep the Property   ☐ Sell the Property

The property is my: ☐ Primary Residence ☐ Second Home   ☐ Investment

The property is: ☐ Owner Occupied   ☐ Renter Occupied   ☐ Vacant

Mailing address:

Property address (if same as mailing address, just write "same"):   E-mail address:

Is the property listed for sale?:   ☐ Yes   ☐ No
Have you received an offer on the property?:   ☐ Yes   ☐ No
Date of Offer: _____ Amount of offer: _____
Agent's Name: _____
Agent's Phone Number: _____
For Sale by Owner?:   ☐ Yes   ☐ No

Have you contacted a credit-counseling agency for help? ☐ Yes   ☐ No
If yes, please complete the following:
Counselor's Name: _____
Agency Name: _____
Counselor's Phone Number: _____
Counselor's E-mail: _____

Who pays the real estate tax bill on your property?
☐ I do   ☐ Lender does   ☐ Paid by condo or HOA
Are the taxes current?   ☐ Yes   ☐ No
Condominium or HOA Fees?   ☐ Yes   ☐ No $ _____
Paid to: _____

Who pays the hazard insurance premium for your property?
☐ I do   ☐ Lender does   ☐ Paid by condo or HOA
Is the policy current?   ☐ Yes   ☐ No
Name of Insurance Co.: _____
Insurance Co. Phone Number: _____

Have you filed for bankruptcy?   ☐ Yes   ☐ No   If yes: ☐ Chapter 7   ☐ Chapter 13   Filing Date: _____
Has your bankruptcy been discharged?   ☐ Yes   ☐ No   Bankruptcy case number: _____

Additional Liens/Mortgages or Judgments on this property:

Lien holder's Name/Servicer	Balance	Phone Number	Loan Number

INFORMATION ONLY

HARDSHIP AFFIDAVIT

I (We) am/are requesting review under the Making Home Affordable program.
I am having difficulty making my monthly payment because of financial difficulties created by (check all that apply):

☐ My household income has been reduced. For example: underemployment, reduced pay or hours, decline in business earnings, death, disability or divorce of a borrower or co-borrower.

☐ My monthly debt payments are excessive and I am overextended with my creditors. Debt includes credit cards, home equity or other debt.

☐ My expenses have increased. For example: monthly mortgage payment reset, high medical or health care costs, uninsured losses, increased utilities or property taxes.

☐ My cash reserves, including all liquid assets, are insufficient to maintain my current mortgage payment and cover basic living expenses at the same time.

☐ My household income has been reduced due to unemployment.

☐ Other:

Explanation (continue on back of page 3 if necessary): _____
_____

These forms are for informational purpose. Please obtain the most updated forms and information by contacting the appropriate lender or visiting their website for instructions.

INFORMATION ONLY

Loan Number: _____

INCOME/EXPENSES FOR HOUSEHOLD		▶ Number of People in Household:	

Monthly Household Income		Monthly Household Expenses/Debt		Household Assets	
Monthly Gross Wages	$	First Mortgage Payment	$	Checking Account(s)	$
Overtime	$	Second Mortgage Payment	$	Checking Account(s)	$
Child Support/Alimony/ Separate Maintenance Income[2]	$	Insurance	$	Savings/Money Market	$
Social Security/SSDI	$	Property Taxes	$	CDs	$
Other monthly income from pensions, annuities or retirement plans	$	Credit Cards/Installment Loan(s) (total minimum payment per month)	$	Stocks/Bonds	$
Tips, commissions, bonus and self-employed income	$	Alimony, child support payments	$	Other Cash on Hand	$
Rents Received	$	Net Rental Expenses	$	Other Real Estate (estimated value)	$
Unemployment Income	$	HOA/Condo Fees/Property Maintenance	$	Other _____	$
Food Stamps/Welfare	$	Car Payments	$	Other _____	$
Other (investment income, royalties, interest, dividends, etc.)	$	Other _____ _____	$	Do not include the value of life insurance or retirement plans when calculating assets (401k, pension funds, annuities, IRAs, Keogh plans, etc.)	
Total Gross Income	**$**	**Total Debt/Expenses**	**$**	**Total Assets**	**$**

INCOME MUST BE DOCUMENTED

[1]Include combined income and expenses from the borrower and co-borrower (if any). If you include income and expenses from a household member who is not a borrower, please specify using the back of this form if necessary.

[2]You are not required to disclose Child Support, Alimony or Separate Maintenance Income, unless you choose to have it considered by your servicer.

INFORMATION FOR GOVERNMENT MONITORING PURPOSES

The following information is requested by the federal government in order to monitor compliance with federal statutes that prohibit discrimination in housing. **You are not required to furnish this information, but are encouraged to do so. The law provides that a lender or servicer may not discriminate either on the basis of this information, or on whether you choose to furnish it.** If you furnish the information, please provide both ethnicity and race. For race, you may check more than one designation. If you do not furnish ethnicity, race, or sex, the lender or servicer is required to note the information on the basis of visual observation or surname if you have made this request for a loan modification in person. **If you do not wish to furnish the information, please check the box below.**

BORROWER ☐ I do not wish to furnish this information	CO-BORROWER ☐ I do not wish to furnish this information
Ethnicity: ☐ Hispanic or Latino ☐ Not Hispanic or Latino	Ethnicity: ☐ Hispanic or Latino ☐ Not Hispanic or Latino
Race: ☐ American Indian or Alaska Native ☐ Asian ☐ Black or African American ☐ Native Hawaiian or Other Pacific Islander ☐ White	Race: ☐ American Indian or Alaska Native ☐ Asian ☐ Black or African American ☐ Native Hawaiian or Other Pacific Islander ☐ White
Sex: ☐ Female ☐ Male	Sex: ☐ Female ☐ Male

To be completed by interviewer

This request was taken by:	Interviewer's Name (print or type) & ID Number	Name/Address of Interviewer's Employer
☐ Face-to-face interview ☐ Mail ☐ Telephone ☐ Internet	Interviewer's Signature Date Interviewer's Phone Number (include area code)	

INFORMATION ONLY

Loan Number: _____

ACKNOWLEDGEMENT AND AGREEMENT

In making this request for consideration under the Making Home Affordable Program I certify under penalty of perjury:

1. That all of the information in this document is truthful and the event(s) identified on page 1 is/are the reason that I need to request a modification of the terms of my mortgage loan, short sale or deed-in-lieu of foreclosure.

2. I understand that the Servicer, the U.S. Department of Treasury, or their agents may investigate the accuracy of my statements and may require me to provide supporting documentation. I also understand that knowingly submitting false information may violate Federal law.

3. I understand the Servicer will pull a current credit report on all borrowers obligated on the Note.

4. I understand that if I have intentionally defaulted on my existing mortgage, engaged in fraud or misrepresented any fact(s) in connection with this document, the Servicer may cancel any Agreement under Making Home Affordable and may pursue foreclosure on my home.

5. That my property is owner-occupied; I have not received a condemnation notice; and there has been no change in the ownership of the Property since I signed the documents for my existing mortgage.

6. I am willing to provide all requested documents and to respond to all Servicer questions in a timely manner.

7. I understand that the Servicer will use the information in this document to evaluate my eligibility for a loan modification or short sale or deed-in-lieu of foreclosure, but the Servicer is not obligated to offer me assistance based solely on the statements in this document.

8. I am willing to commit to credit counseling if it is determined that my financial hardship is related to excessive debt.

9. If I was discharged in a Chapter 7 bankruptcy proceeding subsequent to the execution of the Loan Documents, or am currently entitled to the protections of any automatic stay in bankruptcy, I acknowledge that Servicer is providing the information about the Making Home Affordable program at my request and for informational purposes, and not as an attempt to impose personal liability for the debt evidenced by the Note.

10. I understand that the Servicer will collect and record personal information, including, but not limited to, my name, address, telephone number, social security number, credit score, income, payment history, government monitoring information, and information about account balances and activity. I understand and consent to the disclosure of my personal information and the terms of Making Home Affordable Agreement by Servicer to (a) the U.S. Department of the Treasury; (b) Fannie Mae and Freddie Mac in connection with their responsibilities under the Homeowner Affordability and Stability Plan; (c) any investor, insurer, guarantor or servicer that owns, insures, guarantees or services my first lien or subordinate lien (if applicable) mortgage loan(s); (d) companies that perform support services in conjunction with Making Home Affordable; and (e) any HUD certified housing counselor.

11. I understand that if Servicer offers me a trial period plan under the Making Home Affordable Program, and I fail to accept or complete the trial plan for any reason, including, for example, declining the trial plan offer, failing to accept the trial plan offer, failing to make trial plan payments in a timely manner, or failing to accept a final modification at the end of the trial period, I may permanently lose eligibility for a modification under the Making Home Affordable Program and any other modification program offered by Servicer.

These forms are for informational purpose. Please obtain the most updated forms and information by contacting the appropriate lender or visiting their website for instructions.

Loan Number: _____

_____

BORROWER SIGNATURE

Date: _____ / _____ / _____

_____

CO-BORROWER SIGNATURE

Date: _____ / _____ / _____

HOMEOWNER'S HOTLINE

If you have questions about this document or the modification process, please call your Servicer.
If you have questions about the program that your Servicer cannot answer or need further counseling,
you can call the Homeowner's HOPE™ Hotline at 1-888-995-HOPE (4673). The Hotline can help answer questions
about the program and offers free HUD-certified counseling services in English and Spanish.

NOTICE TO BORROWERS

Be advised that by signing this document you understand that any documents and information you submit to your Servicer in connection with the Making Home Affordable Program are under penalty of perjury. Any misstatement of material fact made in the completion of these documents including by not limited to misstatement regarding the occupancy in your home, hardship circumstances, and/or income, expenses, or assets will subject you to potential criminal investigation and prosecution for the following crimes: perjury, false statements, mail fraud, and wire fraud. The information contained in these documents is subject to examination and verification. Any potential misrepresentation will be referred to the appropriate law enforcement authority for investigation and prosecution. By signing this document, you certify, represent and agree that: "Under penalty of perjury, all documents and information I have provided to Lender in connection with the Making Home Affordable Program, including the documents and information regarding my eligibility for the program, are true and correct."

If you are aware of fraud, waste, abuse mismanagement or misrepresentation affiliated with the Troubled Asset Relief Program, please contact the SIGTARP Hotline by calling 1-877-SIG-2009 (toll-free), 202-622-4559 (fax), or www.sigtarp.gov. Mail can be sent to Hotline Office of the Special Inspector General for Troubled Asset Relief Program, 1801 L St. NW, Washington, DC 20220.

INFORMATION ONLY

These forms are for informational purpose. Please obtain the most updated forms and information by contacting the appropriate lender or visiting their website for instructions.

Form **4506-T**

Request for Transcript of Tax Return

OMB No. 1545-1872

Department of the Treasury
Internal Revenue Service

▶ **Request may be rejected if the form is incomplete or illegible.**

Tip. Use Form 4506-T to order a transcript or other return information free of charge. See the product list below. You can also call 1-800-829-1040 to order a transcript. If you need a copy of your return, use **Form 4506, Request for Copy of Tax Return.** There is a fee to get a copy of your return.

1a Name shown on tax return. If a joint return, enter the name shown first.	**1b** First social security number on tax return or employer identification number (see instructions)
2a If a joint return, enter spouse's name shown on tax return.	**2b** Second social security number if joint tax return

3 Current name, address (including apt., room, or suite no.), city, state, and ZIP code

4 Previous address shown on the last return filed if different from line 3

5 If the transcript or tax information is to be mailed to a third party (such as a mortgage company), enter the third party's name, address, and telephone number. The IRS has no control over what the third party does with the tax information.

Regular Mail:
Chase Fulfillment Center
PO Box 469030
Glendale, CO 80246

Overnight Mail:
Chase Fulfillment Center
710 South Ash Street, Suite #200
Glendale, CO 80246

Phone number:
866-233-5320

Caution. *If the transcript is being mailed to a third party, ensure that you have filled in line 6 and line 9 before signing. Sign and date the form once you have filled in these lines. Completing these steps helps to protect your privacy.*

6 **Transcript requested.** Enter the tax form number here (1040, 1065, 1120, etc.) and check the appropriate box below. Enter only one tax form number per request. ▶ _____

a **Return Transcript,** which includes most of the line items of a tax return as filed with the IRS. A tax return transcript does not reflect changes made to the account after the return is processed. Transcripts are only available for the following returns: Form 1040 series, Form 1065, Form 1120, Form 1120A, Form 1120H, Form 1120L, and Form 1120S. Return transcripts are available for the current year and returns processed during the prior 3 processing years. Most requests will be processed within 10 business days . . . . . . ☐

b **Account Transcript,** which contains information on the financial status of the account, such as payments made on the account, penalty assessments, and adjustments made by you or the IRS after the return was filed. Return information is limited to items such as tax liability and estimated tax payments. Account transcripts are available for most returns. Most requests will be processed within 30 calendar days. . ☐

c **Record of Account,** which is a combination of line item information and later adjustments to the account. Available for current year and 3 prior tax years. Most requests will be processed within 30 calendar days . . . . ☐

7 **Verification of Nonfiling,** which is proof from the IRS that you **did not** file a return for the year. Current year requests are only available after June 15th. There are no availability restrictions on prior year requests. Most requests will be processed within 10 business days . . ☐

8 **Form W-2, Form 1099 series, Form 1098 series, or Form 5498 series transcript.** The IRS can provide a transcript that includes data from these information returns. State or local information is not included with the Form W-2 information. The IRS may be able to provide this transcript information for up to 10 years. Information for the current year is generally not available until the year after it is filed with the IRS. For example, W-2 information for 2007, filed in 2008, will not be available from the IRS until 2009. If you need W-2 information for retirement purposes, you should contact the Social Security Administration at 1-800-772-1213. Most requests will be processed within 45 days . . . ☐

Caution. *If you need a copy of Form W-2 or Form 1099, you should first contact the payer. To get a copy of the Form W-2 or Form 1099 filed with your return, you must use Form 4506 and request a copy of your return, which includes all attachments.*

9 **Year or period requested.** Enter the ending date of the year or period, using the mm/dd/yyyy format. If you are requesting more than four years or periods, you must attach another Form 4506-T. For requests relating to quarterly tax returns, such as Form 941, you must enter each quarter or tax period separately.

_____   _____   _____   _____

Signature of taxpayer(s). I declare that I am either the taxpayer whose name is shown on line 1a or 2a, or a person authorized to obtain the tax information requested. If the request applies to a joint return, **either** husband or wife must sign. If signed by a corporate officer, partner, guardian, tax matters partner, executor, receiver, administrator, trustee, or party other than the taxpayer, I certify that I have the authority to execute Form 4506-T on behalf of the taxpayer. **Note.** *For transcripts being sent to a third party, this form must be received within 120 days of signature date.*

Telephone number of taxpayer on line 1a or 2a

Sign Here

▶ Signature (see instructions)   Date

▶ Title (if line 1a above is a corporation, partnership, estate, or trust)

▶ Spouse's signature   Date

For Privacy Act and Paperwork Reduction Act Notice, see page 2.   Cat. No. 37667N   Form **4506-T**

General Instructions

Purpose of form. Use Form 4506-T to request tax return information. You can also designate a third party to receive the information. See line 5.

Tip. Use Form 4506, Request for Copy of Tax Return, to request copies of tax returns.

Where to file. Mail or fax Form 4506-T to the address below for the state you lived in, or the state your business was in, when that return was filed. There are two address charts: one for individual transcripts (Form 1040 series and Form W-2) and one for all other transcripts.

If you are requesting more than one transcript or other product and the chart below shows two different RAIVS teams, send your request to the team based on the address of your most recent return.

Automated transcript request. You can call 1-800-829-1040 to order a transcript through the automated self-help system. Follow prompts for "questions about your tax account" to order a tax return transcript.

Chart for individual transcripts (Form 1040 series and Form W-2)

If you filed an individual return and lived in:	Mail or fax to the "Internal Revenue Service" at:
Florida, Georgia, North Carolina, South Carolina	RAIVS Team P.O. Box 47-421 Stop 91 Doraville, GA 30362
	770-455-2335
Alabama, Kentucky, Louisiana, Mississippi, Tennessee, Texas, a foreign country, or A.P.O. or F.P.O. address	RAIVS Team Stop 6716 AUSC Austin, TX 73301
	512-460-2272
Alaska, Arizona, California, Colorado, Hawaii, Idaho, Illinois, Indiana, Iowa, Kansas, Michigan, Minnesota, Montana, Nebraska, Nevada, New Mexico, North Dakota, Oklahoma, Oregon, South Dakota, Utah, Washington, Wisconsin, Wyoming	RAIVS Team Stop 37106 Fresno, CA 93888
	559-456-5876
Arkansas, Connecticut, Delaware, District of Columbia, Maine, Maryland, Massachusetts, Missouri, New Hampshire, New Jersey, New York, Ohio, Pennsylvania, Rhode Island, Vermont, Virginia, West Virginia	RAIVS Team Stop 6705 P-6 Kansas City, MO 64999
	816-292-6102

Chart for all other transcripts

If you lived in or your business was in:	Mail or fax to the "Internal Revenue Service" at:
Alabama, Alaska, Arizona, Arkansas, California, Colorado, Florida, Hawaii, Idaho, Iowa, Kansas, Louisiana, Minnesota, Mississippi, Missouri, Montana, Nebraska, Nevada, New Mexico, North Dakota, Oklahoma, Oregon, South Dakota, Tennessee, Texas, Utah, Washington, Wyoming, a foreign country, or A.P.O. or F.P.O. address	RAIVS Team P.O. Box 9941 Mail Stop 6734 Ogden, UT 84409
	801-620-6922
Connecticut, Delaware, District of Columbia, Georgia, Illinois, Indiana, Kentucky, Maine, Maryland, Massachusetts, Michigan, New Hampshire, New Jersey, New York, North Carolina, Ohio, Pennsylvania, Rhode Island, South Carolina, Vermont, Virginia, West Virginia, Wisconsin	RAIVS Team P.O. Box 145500 Stop 2800 F Cincinnati, OH 45250
	859-669-3592

Line 1b. Enter your employer identification number (EIN) if your request relates to a business return. Otherwise, enter the first social security number (SSN) shown on the return. For example, if you are requesting Form 1040 that includes Schedule C (Form 1040), enter your SSN.

Line 6. Enter only one tax form number per request.

Signature and date. Form 4506-T must be signed and dated by the taxpayer listed on line 1a or 2a. If you completed line 5 requesting the information be sent to a third party, the IRS must receive Form 4506-T within 120 days of the date signed by the taxpayer or it will be rejected.

Individuals. Transcripts of jointly filed tax returns may be furnished to either spouse. Only one signature is required. Sign Form 4506-T exactly as your name appeared on the original return. If you changed your name, also sign your current name.

Corporations. Generally, Form 4506-T can be signed by: (1) an officer having legal authority to bind the corporation, (2) any person designated by the board of directors or other governing body, or (3) any officer or employee on written request by any principal officer and attested to by the secretary or other officer.

Partnerships. Generally, Form 4506-T can be signed by any person who was a member of the partnership during any part of the tax period requested on line 9.

All others. See Internal Revenue Code section 6103(e) if the taxpayer has died, is insolvent, is a dissolved corporation, or if a trustee, guardian, executor, receiver, or administrator is acting for the taxpayer.

Documentation. For entities other than individuals, you must attach the authorization document. For example, this could be the letter from the principal officer authorizing an employee of the corporation or the Letters Testamentary authorizing an individual to act for an estate.

Privacy Act and Paperwork Reduction Act Notice. We ask for the information on this form to establish your right to gain access to the requested tax information under the Internal Revenue Code. We need this information to properly identify the tax information and respond to your request. You are not required to request any transcript; if you do request a transcript, sections 6103 and 6109 and their regulations require you to provide this information, including your SSN or EIN. If you do not provide this information, we may not be able to process your request. Providing false or fraudulent information may subject you to penalties.

Routine uses of this information include giving it to the Department of Justice for civil and criminal litigation, and cities, states, and the District of Columbia for use in administering their tax laws. We may also disclose this information to other countries under a tax treaty, to federal and state agencies to enforce federal nontax criminal laws, or to federal law enforcement and intelligence agencies to combat terrorism.

You are not required to provide the information requested on a form that is subject to the Paperwork Reduction Act unless the form displays a valid OMB control number. Books or records relating to a form or its instructions must be retained as long as their contents may become material in the administration of any Internal Revenue law. Generally, tax returns and return information are confidential, as required by section 6103.

The time needed to complete and file Form 4506-T will vary depending on individual circumstances. The estimated average time is: **Learning about the law or the form,** 10 min.; **Preparing the form,** 12 min.; and **Copying, assembling, and sending the form to the IRS,** 20 min.

If you have comments concerning the accuracy of these time estimates or suggestions for making Form 4506-T simpler, we would be happy to hear from you. You can write to the Internal Revenue Service, Tax Products Coordinating Committee, SE:W:CAR:MP:T:T:SP, 1111 Constitution Ave. NW, IR-6526, Washington, DC 20224. Do not send the form to this address. Instead, see *Where to file* on this page.

HELP FOR AMERICA'S HOMEOWNERS.

MAKING HOME AFFORDABLE sm

Dodd-Frank Certification

The following information is requested by the federal government in accordance with the Dodd-Frank Wall Street Reform and Consumer Protection Act (Pub. L. 111-203). You are required to furnish this information. The law provides that no person shall be eligible to begin receiving assistance from the Making Home Affordable Program, authorized under the Emergency Economic Stabilization Act of 2008 (12 U.S.C. 5201 et seq.), or any other mortgage assistance program authorized or funded by that Act, if such person, in connection with a mortgage or real estate transaction, has been convicted, within the last 10 years, of any one of the following: (A) felony larceny, theft, fraud, or forgery, (B) money laundering or (C) tax evasion.

I/we certify under penalty of perjury that I/we have not been convicted within the last 10 years of any one of the following in connection with a mortgage or real estate transaction:

    (a) felony larceny, theft, fraud, or forgery,
    (b) money laundering or
    (c) tax evasion.

I/we understand that the servicer, the U.S. Department of the Treasury, or their agents may investigate the accuracy of my statements by performing routine background checks, including automated searches of federal, state and county databases, to confirm that I/we have not been convicted of such crimes. I/we also understand that knowingly submitting false information may violate Federal law.

This Certificate is effective on the earlier of the date listed below or the date received by your servicer.

_____   _____
Borrower Signature   Date

_____   _____
Co-Borrower Signature   Date

_____   _____
Co-Borrower Signature   Date

_____   _____
Co-Borrower Signature   Date

Loan #:		
Borrower:	Res. Tel. #:	Work Tel. #:
Social Security Number:		
Co-Borrower:	Res. Tel. #:	Work Tel. #:
Social Security Number:		
Property Address:		
City: State:		Zip Code:
Current Address (if different from property address – do not use post office box):		
City: State:		Zip Code:

Total number of dependents: _____

Have you contacted any HUD-approved credit or housing counselors? _____

Is your home listed for sale? _____

If yes, who is your agent? _____

Borrower Employment History	Co-Borrower Employment History
Currently Employed? ☐ Yes ☐ No	Currently Employed? ☐ Yes ☐ No
How Long? _____	How Long? _____
Present Employer:	Present Employer:
Address:	Address:
Phone No.	Phone No.
Contact Supervisor:	Contact Supervisor:
Position/Title:	Position/Title:
If self-employed, name of	If self-employed, name of
co.:	co.:

INFORMATION ONLY

Description	Monthly Income		Total
	Borrower	Co-Borrower	
Social Security Income			
Gross Salary/Wages	$	$	$ 0.00
Unemployment Income (Benefit end date:)	$	$	$ 0.00
Child Support/Alimony	$	$	$ 0.00
Disability Income	$	$	$ 0.00
Rental Income	$	$	$ 0.00
Interest/Dividend Income	$	$	$ 0.00

ASSETS/LIABILITIES – If you own real estate in addition to your personal residence, or if your personal residence is subject to one or more junior mortgages, attach a complete list of property addresses (if different from personal residence), name(s) of lender, lender's address and phone number, account numbers, monthly payment, amount owed, and estimated value & rental income.

Description	Estimated Value	Amount Owed	Net Value
Personal Residence	$	$	$
Personal Property	$	$	$
Checking Accounts	$	$	$
Savings Accounts	$	$	$
IRA/401k/Keogh Accounts	$	$	$
Stocks/Bonds/CD's	$	$	$
Cash Value of Life Insurance	$	$	$
Other	$	$	$
Totals	$ 0.00	$ 0.00	$ 0.00

EXPENSES

	Liabilities			Expenses	
	Creditor Name	**Payment**	**Balance**		**Monthly Payment**
Other Mortgages/Liens/Rents		$	$	Auto Gasoline	$
Other Murtgages/Liens/Rents		$	$	Auto Insurance (monthly amount)	$
Other Mortgages/Liens/Rents		$	$	Utilities/Water	$
Other Mortgages/Liens/Rents		$	$	Utilities/Sewer	$
Property Taxes		$	$	Utilities/Phone	$
Homeowner's Insurance		$	$	Utilities/Gas/Oil	$
Flood Insurance (if applicable)		$	$	Utilities/Electric	$
Homeowner's Association Dues		$	$	Food	$
Alimony/Child Support		$	$	State and/or Federal Tax Liens	$
Child Care		$	$	Other (describe):	$
Health Insurance (if nor deducted from wages)		$	$	Other (describe):	$
Life Insurance Premiums (if separate policy)		$	$	Other (describe):	$
Uninsured Medical/Dental Expenses		$	$		
Credit Card/Installment Loans		$	$		
Credit Card/Installment Loans		$	$		
Credit Card/Installment Loans		$			
Credit Card/Installment Loans		$	$		
Student Loans		$	$		
Auto Loan(s)		$	$		
Auto Lease		$	$		

Property Condition

I certify the condition of the property is as noted below (circle one):

1-Excellent   2-Good   3-Fair   4-Poor   5-Condemned   6-Inaccessible

Have you ever received a Condemnation Notice? ☐ Yes ☐ No

Real Estate Taxes

Do you receive and pay the Real Estate Tax bill on your home or does your lender pay it for you?

☐ I do   ☐ Lender does

Are the taxes current? ☐ Yes ☐ No

If you pay it, provide a copy of your tax statement.

Hazard Insurance

Do you pay for a hazard insurance policy? ☐ Yes ☐ No

Is the policy current? ☐ Yes ☐ No

If you pay it, provide a copy of the policy.

INFORMATION ONLY

I have described my present financial condition on this financial analysis form and have attached required documentation. Under my present circumstances, I cannot bring my mortgage loan current or I soon may become delinquent due to financial hardship. Therefore, I hereby request assistance from ████████████████████████████ ("Servicer") under its loss mitigation program.

If Servicer determines that the information and/or documentation I have provided with this financial analysis form is incomplete, or insufficient to render a decision as to my eligibility for loss mitigation, my request for loss mitigation may be denied or delayed until I have provided Servicer with additional information and/or documentation as requested. If I have misrepresented any information and/or documentation, I understand and agree that such misrepresentation will be grounds either for immediate rejection of my request for assistance or immediate termination of any loss mitigation agreed to by Servicer. Furthermore, I shall be liable for any losses or damages suffered by Servicer as a result of such misrepresentation.

In the event a third party is designated to act on my behalf, I have included written authorization to the designee to act on my behalf. In the event I am able to bring the loan current or am able to sell the property for an amount sufficient to pay off my mortgage loan in full during the evaluation process, I understand that my request for participation in Servicer's loss mitigation program will be withdrawn without further action.

By signing below, I declare that the information provided above is true and correct to the best of my knowledge and fully understand that knowingly making a false statement concerning such information may constitute a crime punishable by fine, imprisonment, or both.

_____   _____
Signature of Borrower   Date

_____   _____
Signature of Borrower   Date

INFORMATION ONLY

_____   _____
Signature of Borrower   Date

_____   _____
Signature of Borrower   Date

REMINDER

Before mailing, make sure that all borrowers on the mortgage note have signed and dated this form. Also, include documentation as noted below.

1. Signed Hardship Explanation Letter.
2. Source(s) of monthly income and proof of the amount:
   - **Wage Earners** – All pay stubs covering the most recent full month.
   - **Self-Employment** – Borrower signed a) Profit & loss statement covering the most recently past 6 months, or b) Federal tax returns for the past year.
   - **Social Security Retirement Disability** – Most recent benefit letter dated/issued within the last 12 months.
   - **Unemployment Benefits** – Benefit statement/letter confirming benefit amount.
   - **Boarder or Family Contributions** – Signed letter from the paying party.
   - **Family, Alimony, Child Support** – Signed letter from the paying party or copy of the court order.
   - **Rents** – Rental Agreement(s).

████████████████████████████, is a debt collector. However, in the event the recipient has been discharged pursuant to or is under the protection of federal bankruptcy law, this correspondence is being provided solely for informational purposes and does not constitute and should not be construed as an attempt to collect a debt.

APPENDIX B: HELPFUL LINKS

HELPFUL ORGANIZATIONAL LINKS

http://portal.hud.gov/hudportal/HUD?src=/topics/avoiding_foreclosure

http://www.nw.org/network/foreclosure/nfmcp/EHLPconsumers.asp

http://www.treasury.gov/initiatives/financial-stability/programs/housing-programs/Pages/default.aspx

http://portal.hud.gov/hudportal/HUD?src=/program_offices/housing/sfh/nsc/nschome

http://www.hopenow.com

HELPFUL LENDER LINKS

https://www.chase.com/chf/mortgage/hrm_resources

http://homeloanhelp.bankofamerica.com/en/index.html?cm_mmc=CRE-Mortgage-_-vanity-_-MO01VN001O_mhahomeloanhelp-_-Online

http://homeloanhelp.bankofamerica.com/en/short-sale-process.html

https://www.wellsfargo.com/homeassist/

https://www.wellsfargo.com/homeassist/shortsale

https://www.ahmsi3.com/servicing/BAT_ba.asp

https://www.suntrustmortgage.com/

https://www.citimortgage.com/Mortgage/Home.do?page=homeowner_assistance

https://www.gmacmortgage.com/finform/hhstart.htm

APPENDIX C: HELPFUL LENDER CONTACT INFORMATION

American Home Mortgage	877-304-3100
AmTrust Bank	888-696-4444
Bank of America	800-669-6607
Beneficial	800-333-5848
Chase	800-446-8939
CitiFinancial Mortgage	800-753-3673
Citimortgage	800-283-7918
Countrywide / Bank of America	800-262-4218
EMC Mortgage	888-609-2379
Fifth Third Bank	800-375-1745
First Merit Bank	888-728-9931
GMAC Mortgage	800-850-4622
HSBC Mortgage	800-338-6441
Huntington National Bank	800-323-4695
Key Bank	800-422-2442
Mortgage Electronic Registration Systems	888-679-6377
Ocwen Federal Bank	800-746-2936
PNC Mortgage	800-367-9305
Select Portfolio Servicing	888-818-6032
Third Federal Savings	888-844-7333
US Bank	800-365-7900
Wachovia Bank / Well Fargo	866-642-8608
Washington Mutual	866-926-8937
Wells Fargo	877-216-8448